Be an eco hero

At home

Sue Barraclough

FRANKLIN WATTS

LONDON • SYDNEY

This edition 2012

Franklin Watts
338 Euston Road
London NW1 3BH

Franklin Watts Australia
Level 17/207 Kent Street
Sydney, NSW 2000

Series editor: Sarah Peutrill
Art director: Jonathan Hair
Design: Robert Walster, Big Blu Design
Illustrator: Gary Swift

Dewey number: 640

ISBN 978 1 4451 0716 5

Printed in China

Franklin Watts is a division of
Hachette Children's Books, an
Hachette UK company.
www.hachette.co.uk

Credits: Anyka/istockphoto: 14bl. Timur Arbaev/istockphoto: 14cr. Gerald Barnard/istockphoto: 16r. Todd Bates/Istockphoto: 23c. Martin Carlsson/istockphoto: 11b. Tye Carnelli/istockphoto: 24b. Yvonne Chamberlain/istockphoto: 6t. Kimberley Deprey/istockphoto: 21t. Elena Elisseeva /Shutterstock: 19cl. Elnur/Shutterstock: 25l. EML/Shutterstock: 10r. Mandy Godbehear/istockphoto: 18b. Kim Gunkel/istockphoto: 13bl. Hallgerd/Shutterstock: 19b. Andrew Hill/istockphoto: 15br. J Hindman/Shutterstock: 16l. Justin Horrocks/istockphoto: 13tc. Image Source/Corbis: 8t. istockphoto: 23b. Maksym Kravtsov/istockphoto: 15bl. Andrey Kuzmin /Shutterstock: 10l. Edyta Luiek/istockphoto: 19t. Mona Mekela/istockphoto: 25cl. Jim Mills/istockphoto: 23t. Monkey Business Images/Shutterstock: 19cr. Juriah Mosin/Shutterstock: 6b, 13br. Ramplett/istockphoto: front cover, 25cr. RAT87/Shutterstock: 25b. Morley Read/istockphoto: 9. runamock/istockphoto: 17. Nassyrov Ruslan/Shutterstock: 13tl. Jorge Salcedo/istockphoto: 14tr. Kristian Sekulic /istockphoto: 8b. Nina Shannon/istockphoto: 15t. sonyat/istockphoto: 22. Studio Araminta/Shutterstock: 25tr. Tihis/Shutterstock: 13tr. Deniz Unlusu/istockphoto: 18tl. Wishlist Images: 7, 20, 26, 27. Feng Yu/Shutterstock: 25tc. Sergey Zavalnyuk/istockphoto: 21b. Every attempt has been made to clear copyright. Should there be any inadvertent omission please apply to the publisher for rectification.

Contents

Find out ways to help your planet in this book and become an eco hero like me!

Words in **bold** are in the glossary on page 28.

At home

Our homes are full of things that use **energy**. We use **gas** for cooking and for heating our homes. We use **electricity** for lights and to make machines work.

We use water in lots of ways around the home too. We use it for baths, showers, toilets and cleaning cars.

Think of all the things we have in our homes, from furniture to **packaging**, TVs to clothes. All these things are made using energy.

Energy and water are very important to us. Eco heroes don't waste them!

Using energy

We all use a lot of energy such as electricity in our homes every day. Think of all the things we do that use electricity.

All around you there are many other homes using energy too. So if we all save energy, it can make a big difference.

Why save energy?

Most energy is **generated** by burning **fossil fuels,** such as coal. Electricity is generated in **power stations** and travels along power lines like these to our homes.

Power lines

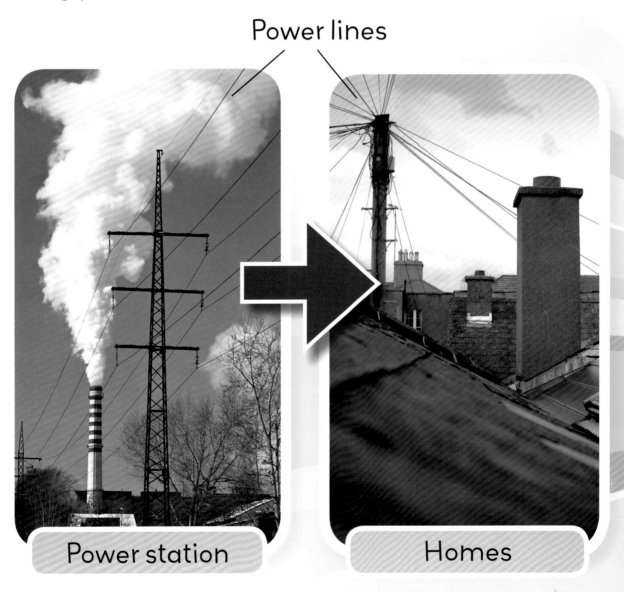

Power station

Homes

Fossil fuels will not last forever and we are using them up quickly. Burning fossil fuels also fills the air with dangerous gases.

You can be an eco hero by using less energy. For example, you can help to choose light bulbs that are energy **efficient**. This means they use less energy and last much longer.

Saving energy

There are lots of easy ways to save energy.

Be an eco hero by:

- Wearing warm clothes and turning down heating to save energy.
- Switching off lights in empty rooms.
- Not leaving TVs, CD players and other items on standby.
- Reading a book or playing a game instead of watching TV.
- Switching off and unplugging mobile phone chargers when not in use.

Unplug

Switch off

Turn off

Wear warm clothes

Read a book

Using water

We all use a lot of water in our homes every day. Think about all the things you do every day that use water.

Washing hands

Drinking water

Flushing the toilet

Can you think of ways to use less water?

Cleaning teeth

Boiling the kettle

Watering the garden

15

Why save water?

Water falls from the sky as rain. It is stored in lakes and **reservoirs**. It is cleaned and pumped along pipes to taps in our homes. This takes energy.

Rainwater

Tap

Clean, fresh water is **precious**. But, the number of people who live on the planet is growing. We all have to share the supply of water. When there is not enough rain some places can get **droughts.**

If we all save water, it can make a big difference. You can be an eco hero by saving water at home.

Saving water

Be an eco hero by:

• Asking an adult to mend dripping taps. A dripping tap wastes four **litres** of water every day.

• Using a bucket to wash the car, not a hose.

• Using a watering can, not a hose to water plants.

• Filling the dishwasher: one full load uses less water than several small ones.

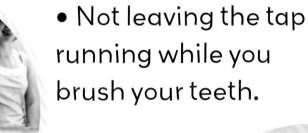

• Not leaving the tap running while you brush your teeth.

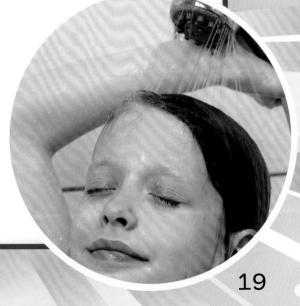

• Having a short shower instead of a bath.

Why reduce, reuse, recycle?

Everything we buy and use is made using energy. Glass, plastic, paper, food, toys, clothes, books and machines are all made using energy and **raw materials**.

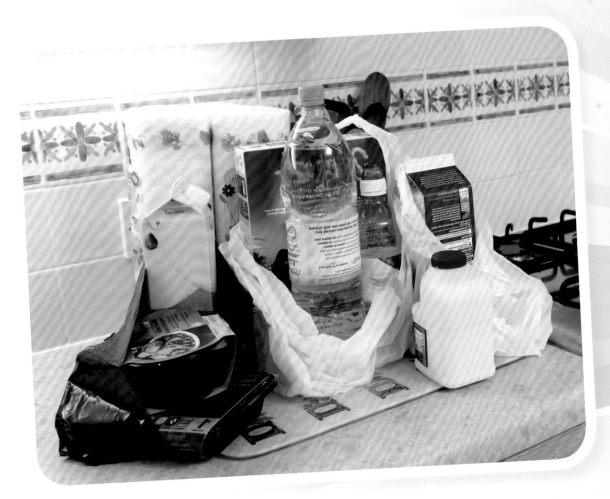

Factories use energy and make pollution.

Reducing waste, **reusing** and **recycling** means:
• less energy and raw materials are used
• less **pollution**
• less rubbish going to **landfill sites.**

Our landfill sites are almost full.

Reducing waste

Reducing waste means shopping carefully so you have less rubbish to throw away at home.

Be an eco hero by:

- Choosing things with less packaging.

Buy loose fruit and vegetables.

Refill bottles.

• Choosing to use refillable drinks bottles.

• Taking your own bags to the shops.

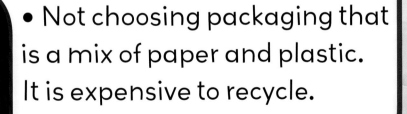

Reuse bags.

• Choosing packaging such as glass or paper that can be recycled easily.

• Not choosing packaging that is a mix of paper and plastic. It is expensive to recycle.

Avoid cartons if you can.

Reuse and recycle

You can also save energy by reusing things and recycling. Reusing something makes the most of the time, energy, materials and money used to make it. Reusing and recycling cuts down pollution and often saves water too.

Be an eco hero and reuse things:

- Repair and repaint before you replace.
- Give old toys and clothes to charity shops.
- Choose reusables not **disposables**.

Give to charity.

Be an eco hero by recycling. All these things can be recycled.

Metal cans and tins

Glass bottles and jars

Some plastics

Food waste

Paper and card

Eco hero activities

Here are some ideas that will make your home fit for an eco hero:

Stop the draughts! Reuse some old socks to make a draught excluder like this. Ask an adult to help.

Stuff old socks with shredded newspaper.

How do the temperatures differ in your house? Which rooms and walls are cooler and which warmer? Use a thermometer to find out. You could put draught excluders in the coldest rooms.

Get crafty! Think of ways to reuse things. You could turn cereal boxes into magazine racks by covering them in used wrapping paper.

Glossary

disposable   an item that is made to be thrown away after it is used.

drought   a long period of time when there is very little rain.

efficient   something that works quickly and well.

electricity   form of energy that makes heat or light that can also be used to make machines work.

energy   something that makes things work, move or change.

fossil fuel   materials found deep under the ground and formed over millions of years from dead animals and plants.

fuel   material used to make heat or light, usually by being burned. Coal, gas and oil are types of fuel.

gas   air-like substance that you cannot see.

generate   to produce energy in a certain form.

landfill site   a huge hole in the ground where rubbish is buried.

litre   a unit for measuring a liquid or gas.

packaging   bottles, packets and boxes used to keep food and other products safe and fresh.

pollution   substance that dirties or poisons air, earth or water.

power station   a factory that generates electricity.

precious   something that has great value because it is rare, expensive or important.

raw material   substance such as wood or oil that is used to make things.

recycling   using materials again or make them into something new.

reservoir   a large lake used to store water.

reusing   using something again.

Learn more

This book shows you some of the ways you can be an eco hero. But there is plenty more you can do to save the planet. Here are some websites that have lots of ideas and information to help you learn more about being an eco hero:

www.foe.co.uk/learning/index.html
Friends of the Earth: 'Green up your life' has lots of information and ideas on how to make a difference.

www.ecokids.ca/pub/eco_info/topics/water/water/index.cfm
Read the Story of Water and find out why it is important to save it.

www.recyclenow.com
Website with recycling news and tips for reducing your waste.

www.theplanetpatrol.com
Find out all about global warming and the things we can all do to tackle it.

Note to parents and teachers: Every effort has been made by the Publishers to ensure that these websites are suitable for children, that they are of the highest educational value, and that they contain no inappropriate or offensive material. However, because of the nature of the Internet, it is impossible to guarantee that the contents of these sites will not be altered. We strongly advise that Internet access is supervised by a responsible adult.

Index